Understanding
CHINA
through Comics

Jing Liu

Volume Three

The Five Dynasties and Ten Kingdoms through
the Yuan Dynasty under Mongol rule

907 - 1368

First Published: April 2013

ISBN: 978-0-9838308-5-6

To Sara, Elizabeth,

Malcolm and Connor,

Katelyn and Yifu,

and many, many more

children who have been born

with a connection to China.

Contents

Introduction

After the fall of the Tang Dynasty, China entered the Five Dynasties and Ten Kingdoms period.

In north China, former Tang military governors fought for supremacy, resulting in five dynasties that quickly succeeded one another. In the south, local warlords established a dozen kingdoms.

During the civil war, northern tribes took up strategic positions in north China, leaving the succeeding Song Dynasty under constant nomadic threats. In response, the Song Chinese built the world's largest standing army and navy, supported by technological breakthroughs and a revolutionized economy.

Waves of northern tribes came, each time more powerful and brutal. In turn, the Song lost the Great Wall region to the Liao Khitans, access to the Silk Roads to the Xia Tanguts, north China to the Jin Jurchens, and finally the entire country to the Yuan Mongols.

Chinese intellectuals were deeply concerned about the military setbacks. But what disturbed them the most was how willing people were to submit to foreign rule. In an effort to save the country and defend its culture, Chinese thinkers initiated a philosophical movement to define what makes the Chinese 'Chinese', which still resonates in Chinese society to this day.

PREVIOUSLY IN

Understanding
CHINA
through Comics

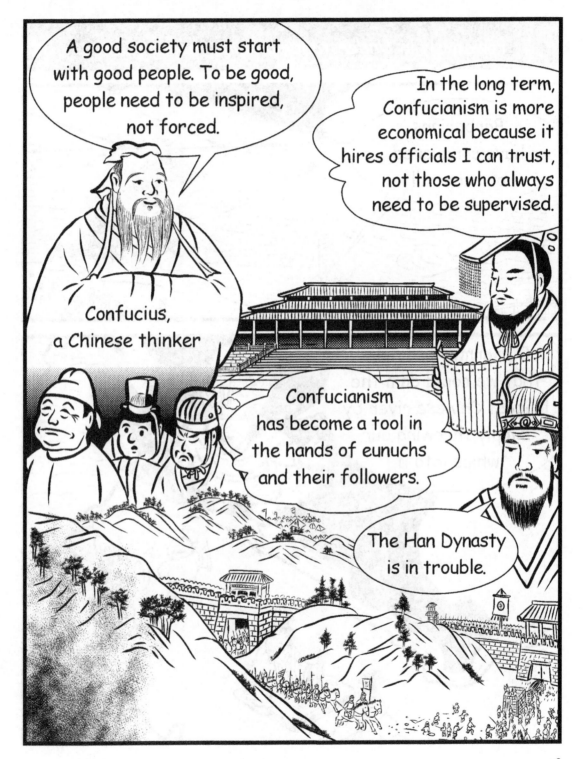

In north China, millions of commoners faced constant threats.

war

heavy taxation

military conscription

hard labor

In this time of widespread suffering, Buddhism, a religion from a foreign land, offered a remedy that was radically different from the Chinese solutions.

Why is there so much suffering?

Confucianism:

We will build a good government to end the suffering.

Taoism:

Suffering is an inescapable aspect of human life, learn to live with it.

Buddhism:

Yes, suffering is part of life, but you can end it.

Practice spiritual exercises to detach yourself from desire, which is the source of suffering.

After nearly 4 centuries of fragmentation, China was unified under the brief but crucial Sui Dynasty, which was succeeded by the more famous Tang Dynasty.

Tang

Of all the Chinese dynasties, the Tang still holds an important record: It was the No. 1 world power.

Disintegration of the late Tang

The massive An Shi rebellion forever changed the political landscape of Tang China.

Over 40 military governors gained autonomy after helping the court crush the rebels.

The most powerful governor had over 90,000 soldiers and 10,000 horses.

A minor one might have had 15,000 men without cavalry.

The Tang government withdrew from regional economies and politics, bringing unintended benefits to local developments.

Now we only pay local taxes, no more national tax for an expensive central government.

We can access many businesses previously monopolized by the state.

The military governors encouraged all sorts of trade.

More business = more tax income = more military spending = more troops to defend my region

The Huang Chao rebellion lasted 10 years, wiping out the entire Chinese aristocracy, the foundation of the Tang Dynasty's ruling elites.

The composition of military governors changed from nobles and scholars to thugs and warriors.

When a powerful warlord, Zhu Wen, replaced the Tang with his Later Liang Dynasty in 907, other Tang governors simply continued to rule on their own.

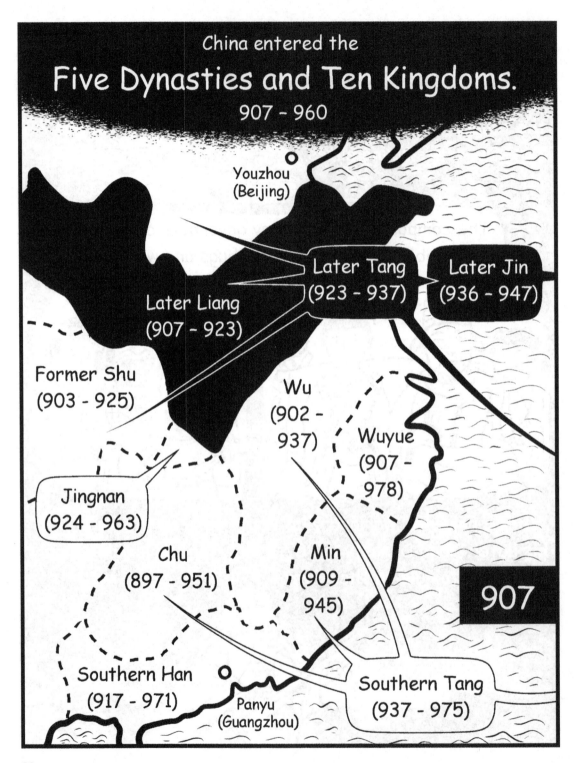

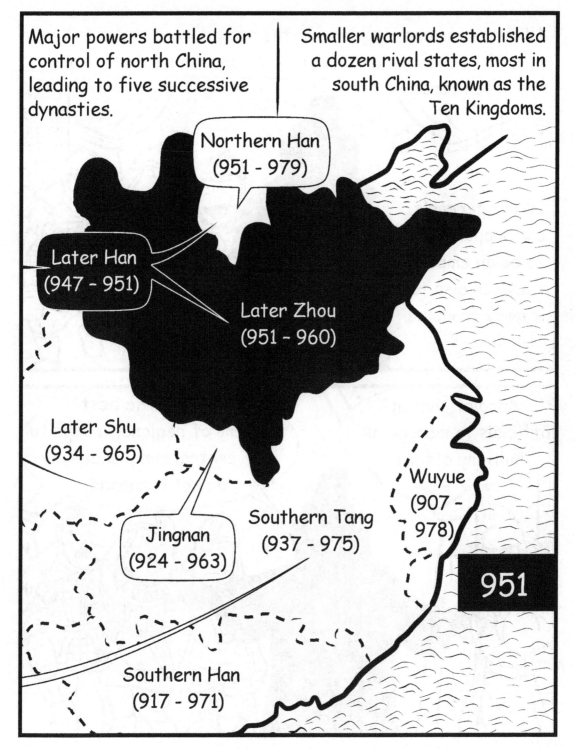

Major powers battled for control of north China, leading to five successive dynasties.

Smaller warlords established a dozen rival states, most in south China, known as the Ten Kingdoms.

Northern Han (951 - 979)

Later Han (947 – 951)

Later Zhou (951 – 960)

Later Shu (934 - 965)

Jingnan (924 - 963)

Southern Tang (937 - 975)

Wuyue (907 - 978)

951

Southern Han (917 - 971)

All dynasties and kingdoms in the period were under military rule. The relationship between a warlord ruler and his army was often tense.

If the generals can support my claim to be an emperor, they can also take it away from me.

Appoint civilian officials to manage all military affairs.

Promote the best soldiers of regional troops to the central army under my direct command.

Unwilling to pledge loyalty to the court, military leaders constantly sold their allegiance to new contesters to the throne, making it hard for anyone to hold on to power.

The Five Dynasties and Ten Kingdoms had 55 emperors in 53 years.

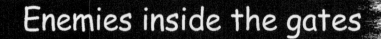

Enemies inside the gates

Making the complicated situation worse, several embattled states sought help from an outside power in Mongolia -- the Khitan tribes.

The Khitans were descendants of a branch of Xianbei nomads who settled in northeast Asia following the fall of the Han Dynasty.

For hundreds of years, they had submitted to their neighbors.

We're surrounded by bullies, and they use our warriors to die for their wars.

In the late 9th century, Khitan's neighboring states were all weakened by civil wars.

The Khitans rose to prominence with the unification of various Khitan tribes in 907.

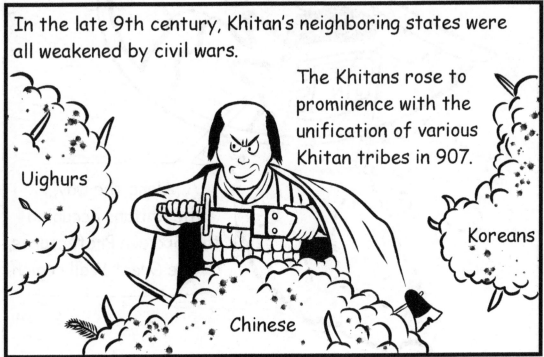

During the Five Dynasties and Ten Kingdoms, the Khitans played a major role in Chinese politics. They pitted warlords against one another, destroying 3 out of 5 dynasties in north China.

Along the way, the Khitans occupied the Sixteen Prefectures, or the Great Wall region.

From then on, the Khitans had a testing locale to gain firsthand experience in agriculture and managing a large population.

It's also a launching ground for our annual raids on China.

After a series of victories in 947, the Khitan state adopted a formal name -- The Liao Dynasty.

Besides the Liao Khitans, another nomadic tribe, the Tanguts, rose in the chaotic time of the late Tang Dynasty.

Tanguts

Khitans

The Tanguts came from multiple ethnic groups including Xianbei people and Tibetans.

A Tangut leader once helped the Tang suppress the Huang Chao rebellion.

For his contribution, the Tang court appointed him as military governor of the Xia prefecture.

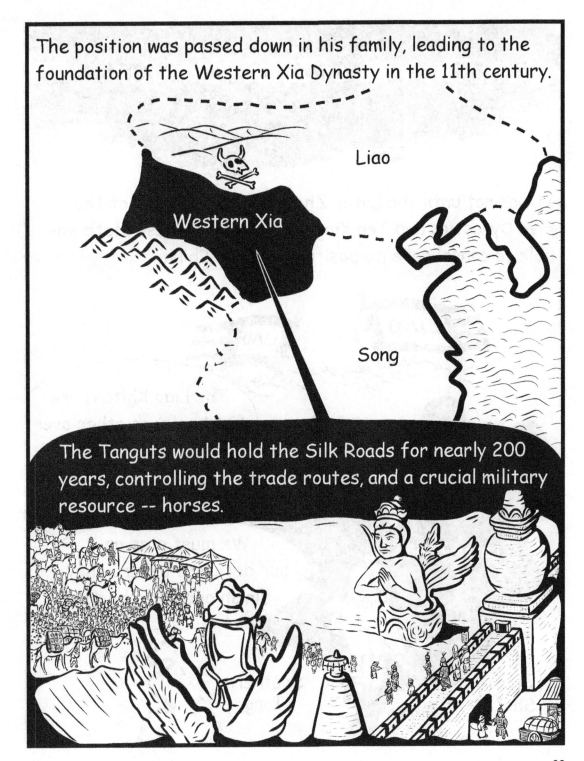

The position was passed down in his family, leading to the foundation of the Western Xia Dynasty in the 11th century.

Liao

Western Xia

Song

The Tanguts would hold the Silk Roads for nearly 200 years, controlling the trade routes, and a crucial military resource -- horses.

The rise of Zhao Kuangyin

It was not until the Later Zhou, the last dynasty of the Five Dynasties and Ten Kingdoms, that a Chinese state was able to consolidate its position in north China.

Sure enough, the Later Zhou soon faced an invasion of the Liao and their ally, the Northern Han.

In 954, the Later Zhou emperor led his men into battle.

Cavalry officer, Zhao Kuangyin, requests permission to speak.

Your Majesty, we ran into the enemy near the city of Gaoping. They're pulling back under our attack.

Chase them!

The emperor led his cavalry, leaving most of his infantry behind.

The right flank
of the Later Zhou army quickly collapsed.
More and more generals fled the battleground.
Thousands of soldiers surrendered.

Facing grave danger,
Zhao Kuangyin charged
forward with 2,000
elite palace troops.

Take out their commander to cause confusion among the enemies!

Zhao fought bravely to resist the flanking enemy force.

Hours passed.

Our reinforcements have arrived!

The Later Zhou won.

The battle marked the first Chinese victory to halt a Khitan incursion following the end of the Tang Dynasty.

The Later Zhou ruler took the chance to tighten control over the army.

Execute 70 commanders on the charge of cowardice!

With the victorious army under centralized command, the Later Zhou carried on successful campaigns against other neighboring states, laying the foundation for the future reunification of China.

The Battle of Gaoping earned Zhao Kuangyin a huge reputation.

Now I promote you as Chief Commander of the Palace Troops.

Six years later in 960, Zhao seized the throne in a coup with support from the army.

Today I declare our state as the Song Dynasty!

The Song Dynasty
960 – 1279

To the Chinese today, the Song Dynasty was one of the most controversial historical periods.

It was a time of economic revolution, rapid urbanization, and spread of knowledge, contributing to the maturity of Chinese philosophy and culture.

But the Song had problems converting its economic and cultural advantages into effective military power to repel constant nomadic threats. Of its 319-year life span, the Song spent nearly 100 years fighting nomads, until its utter destruction.

The Song has replaced the Later Zhou as the most powerful state in China, but we're still not safe.

Several kingdoms allied with the Liao Khitans challenge our position.

We must first reunify China, then deal with the Liao.

Three years after founding, the Song set out on a reunification campaign.

Upon the superior invading force and generous surrender terms, many warlords submitted to the Song.

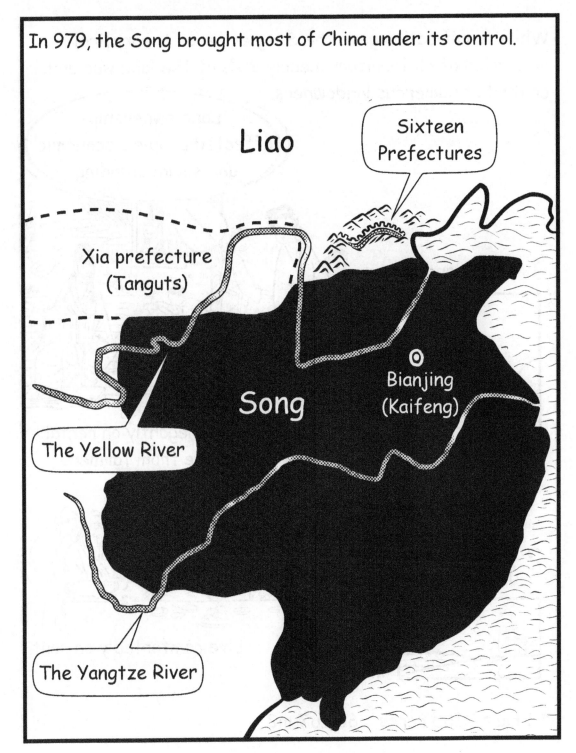

While reunification gave the Song emperor theoretical ownership of all territory, nearly 90% of the land was under control of numerous landowners.

Land ownership affected people's economic and social standing.

1 Large landowners

300 - 10,000 mu* of land

Live elegantly on rental income from farmers.

2 Middle-sized landowners

100 – 300 mu of land

Live comfortably on rent.

* 1 mu = 0.165 acres = 666.67 m2

3 Small landowners
or wealthy farmers

50 – 100
mu of land

Some live on rent to feed
one family, some have to farm.

4 Poor farmers

20 – 50
mu of land

Barely enough land to feed one
family, sometimes rent land.

5 Poorer farmers

1 - 20
mu of land

Not enough land to feed family
so must rent land or work for
large landowners.

6 Poorest farmers

0

Have to work extremely hard but
always live from hand to mouth.

The largest landowners were former warlords of the Five Dynasties and Ten Kingdoms.

The Song allows us to keep our land in exchange for surrendering.

Others included military commanders who were rewarded with farmland for their contribution to the founding of the Song Dynasty...

...and senior officials who received land as a part of their salary.

Large landowners tried to protect their privileges by keeping their children within the ruling class.

During the Song Dynasty, the most standard way to political prominence was through exams.

The imperial examination system had been used for hundreds of years before the Song.

The exam subjects often included Confucian classics and current affairs.

Confucius

Those with high exam scores were eligible to hold office.

It was designed to keep power centralized by preventing any groups from monopolizing government posts.

The first Song emperor, Zhao Kuangyin, expanded the exam system.

After decades of war, the military has gained too much political power.

To replace military rule, the Song must recruit more civil officials through exams.

The Song tried to make the exam system as fair as possible.

Any male adult, regardless of his wealth, can take the exams.

Travel expenses of poor candidates will be paid by the government.

While children of privileged families had advantages in exam preparation, they still had to compete with commoners on the same level.

Kid, I'll make sure you'll have lots of study time, thousands of books, and professional tutors.

But you must study hard to pass the exam, get a good official post, and continue our family legacy.

If you fail, I can use my connection to find you a low level government job, but you'll have little hope for promotion.

The number of exam takers increased dramatically.

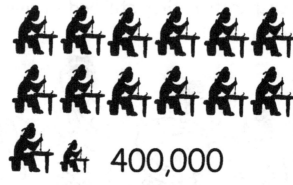

30,000

candidates / year
in the early 11th century
(0.08% of the population)

400,000

candidates / year
in the late 13th century
(1.3% of the population)

The imperial examination system reached its peak in the Song Dynasty.

90% of Song chancellors got their positions through testing, more than in any other Chinese historical period.

In the golden age of the Tang Dynasty, less than 10% of top Tang officials were exam candidates.

The great expansion of imperial examinations led to the triumph of scholar-officials.

Scholar-officials

Aristocrats

Military generals

Religious leaders

Top scholars formed the core of the Song ruling circle, replacing aristocrats, military generals, and religious leaders.

Over 50% of Song scholar-officials were commoners who succeeded in a selection process that was competitive and objective for its time.

The system rewarded talent over birthright, with power passing to the next able candidate.

After years of study for exams, scholar-officials became knowledgeable in philosophy, history, politics, military strategy, diplomacy, literature, and art.

To put these learned men to good use, the Song emperors had a bottom line.

Never put a scholar-official to death no matter how they criticize government policies.

Other dynasties executed outspoken officials by hundreds or even hundreds of thousands.

As a result, the Song had few harsh tyrants, dominating eunuchs, scheming consorts, independent warlords, or massive rebellions -- the usual problems causing the collapse of most Chinese dynasties.

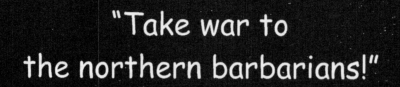

"Take war to the northern barbarians!"

There was an old adversary the Song and its scholarly elites couldn't avoid -- the constant threat from the north. The Song governments decided to wage war on its enemies.

In 979 and 986, the Song launched 2 invasions into Liao territory. Its army reached as far as the Liao Capital.

Liao Southern Capital (Beijing)

But the Liao Khitans were no longer barbarians who lived by hunting, cattle breeding, or moving around in tents. After occupying part of China for decades, they had learned how to organize farmers, store food, and build walled cities to withstand long sieges.

The Song failed miserably in both expeditions.

In one battle, the Song emperor had to escape by disguising himself as a peasant riding a donkey cart.

The Liao retaliated against the Song Chinese.

From annual raids on the Song...

...to a major invasion in 1004.

After rounds of heavy fighting, both sides were too decimated to win.

A peace treaty was signed in 1005.

The Song and Liao will recognize each other as brothers.

The Song will send the Liao an annual tribute: 200,000 bolts of silk and 100,000 ounces of silver.

The Song ambassador to the Liao, Fu Bi, saw the treaty as a good deal.

The annual tribute is less than 2% of what the Song would have spent for military mobilizations against the Liao.

The treaty brought peace to the Song and Liao for over 100 years.

There was a hidden cost.

Unable to recover the natural barrier along the Great Wall region, the Song needed more troops to defend the un-defendable North China plain.

Number of soldiers

The 1004 peace treaty

The first attack on the Liao

The founding of the Song

1,259,000

912,000

666,000

378,000

200,000

Year: 960   980   1000   1020   1040

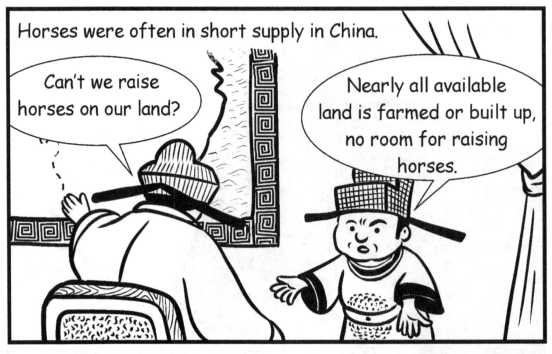

Horses were often in short supply in China.

Can't we raise horses on our land?

Nearly all available land is farmed or built up, no room for raising horses.

Even if we turn some farmland into horse ranches, there is still not enough land for horses to run in, making our horses inferior to those of the nomads.

Where did they get this chicken?

The horse trade couldn't keep up with demand.

The Song had 170,000 warhorses in the beginning.

The number kept dropping due to wars and a blockade by hostile tribes.

At the lowest point in 1102, the Song only had 1,800 horses.

By comparison, the Han Dynasty once had 600,000 horses, and the Tang had 706,000.

The Song must get more horses from Central Asia.

Xia prefecture

Song

The Xia prefecture is the gateway to the region, but it's controlled by a semi-independent Tangut governor.

In 982, the Song put the Xia prefecture under its direct rule.

Appoint a loyal official to govern the Xia and secure our horse supply.

One Tangut tribe rebelled.

At the height of the Song-Liao war, the Tangut rebels sided with the Liao Khitans and quickly gained strength.

In 1038, the Tanguts established their own kingdom, known as the Western Xia Dynasty.

A border war soon broke out.

After years of attrition, the Song and Western Xia agreed to a peace treaty in 1044.

The Western Xia recognizes the Song as its overlord in exchange for receiving an annual gift: 255,000 units of silver, silk, and tea.

Well, it's still cheaper than war.

When we were fighting the Tanguts, our military expense was 18,100,000 units per year!

Western Xia

Population[*]: 3 million

Land: 0.85 million km^2

With wars temporally stopped, China was divided among 3 states.

Army: 0.5 million

Horses: 0.5 million

Song

Population[*] : 125 million

Land: 2.8 million km^2

Army: 1.26 million

Horses: 0.17 million or less

* Population in 1110 AD

Liao

Population[*] : 9 million

Land: around 4.5 million km^2

Army: 0.3 million, over 1 million reserves

Horses: over 1 million

In the following decades, tension remained high among the 3 neighbors.

Increased military expenditures and diplomatic pressures led to the economic stagnation of all dynasties.

Reform ahead of its time

In trying to break out of its stagnation, the Song launched a series of reforms. One prominent reformer was Wang Anshi, a Song chancellor supported by the 18-year-old Emperor Shenzong.

The financial problems demand action now.

Our army has over 1 million men, costing 70% of our tax revenue.

But many are poorly equipped and receive no proper training.

Our resources are vast but our logistics are inefficient.

Our population is large but many live in poverty.

The tax and labor burden imposed on our people is already too great as it is.

Many people can't afford any tax at all.

Today, only 30% of our farmlands are taxable.

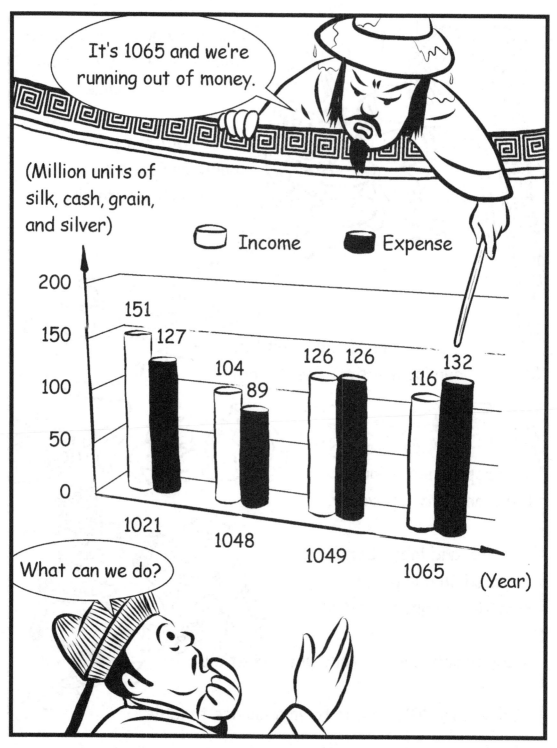

Since farming played the most important role in ancient Chinese economy, a core component of the reform was to improve how farmers worked and lived.

Like all dynasties in the past, our farmers are poor.

Many don't have money to rent farmland or buy seeds and tools to grow food.

They borrow cash from large landlords.

50%

The interest rate is 50%!

The government can start micro-loans to farmers with 20% interest.

20%

The program will work like this.

During planting seasons, a farmer estimates how much surplus he will get at harvest.

Then he takes a loan from the local government.

He spends the money on farming.

After harvest, the farmer repays.

To increase farming productivity, the reformers paid special attention to the cultivation of a new type of food -- rice.

This type of rice has 2 or 3 harvests each year!

Our main staple foods, such as millet and wheat, only have 1 harvest.

The fast-growing rice was first brought to China during the Five Dynasties and Ten Kingdoms.

Min Kingdom

Port of Quanzhou

The new rice could grow anywhere.

To improve irrigation for rice growing, the Song government ordered the construction of more than 10,000 hydraulic projects all over the country.

Before the Song, most dynasties required farmers to provide unpaid labor.

How long do we have to do this?

As long as I say!

Wang Anshi wanted to change this.

The imperial officials can no longer force people to work for free.

Farmers can pay a small fee to avoid labor duty.

Local governments collect the money to pay for services.

While stimulating the economy to increase state income, Wang Anshi also approved radical budget cuts.

The government budget was cut by 40%.

Wang Anshi was eager to use technological innovation to transform the economy, administration, and military.

State-run schools should train more officials with such skills as mathematics, geography, economy, agriculture, medicine, and engineering.

In 10 years, the reformed education provided the government with many technical experts.

Building on achievements from previous dynasties, they made over 100 inventions and put them to practical use.

Astronomical clock for displaying information about stars and planets as well as timekeeping

Watertight compartments in ships

Lifebuoys

Deep drilling for salt

Bellows for blacksmithing

Spinning wheel, both manual and water-driven

Magnifying glass for reading...

The most notable ones accounted for three out of the Four Great Chinese Inventions.*

Gunpowder formula, first recorded in 'Collection of military techniques' by Zeng Gongliang, a scholar-official and supporter of Wang Anshi

武经总要

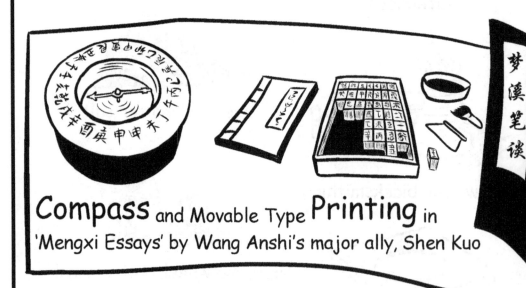

梦溪笔谈

Compass and Movable Type **Printing** in 'Mengxi Essays' by Wang Anshi's major ally, Shen Kuo

* The 4th invention, Paper, came out in 105 AD during the Han Dynasty

The new technologies gave the Song army an edge.

Gunpowder was used in the catapult-launched bomb, the hanging bomb, and the poison-smoke bomb.

We can throw bombs down from city walls at our enemies, especially at fast-moving cavalry.

The compass helped troops navigate in enemy territory.

Before, when we were lost in bad weather or dark nights, we had to let an old horse lead us!

Movable type made printing faster and cheaper.

All the movable characters are reusable.

Manual for army commanders

Teaching material for military academies

After a decade of reform, Emperor Shenzong felt the Song was ready to strike again.

Even after 100 years of existence, the Song still has the disadvantages left by the Five Dynasties and Ten Kingdoms!

We must be free from barbarian threats!

In 1081, an opportunity presented itself.

Your Majesty, the Western Xia ruler tried to retake power from his mother, Empress Liang of Xia, but he failed.

His supporters have rebelled, some asking us for help.

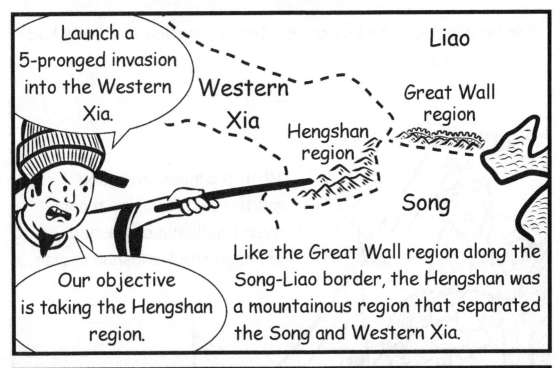

The invasion was the largest military operation the Song had ever launched in its history.

With 5 armies, including militias and logistics troops, over 1 million men pushed through the Hengshan region...

...without knowing a giant trap lay ahead.

Emperor Shenzong was extremely frustrated.

Bad news from the frontline wakes me up in the middle of the night and I walk around my bed till dawn...

Three years after the war, the depressed emperor died at age 37.

Many conservative officials used the military disaster as an excuse to attack Wang Anshi and his reform.

Without Emperor Shenzong's support, the New Policy reform came to an end.

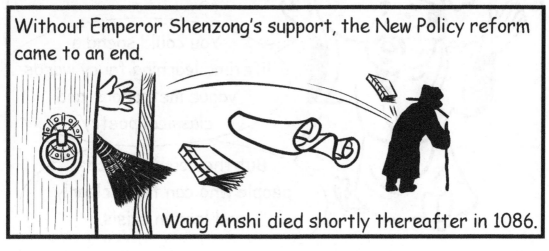

Wang Anshi died shortly thereafter in 1086.

Today, Wang Anshi and his contemporaries are accorded very high regard in China.

They are beacons of Chinese intellectuals.

Fan Zhongyan

Wang Anshi's predecessor, launched a pilot reform to increase administrative efficiency, including cutting corrupt officials.

Ouyang Xiu

Fan Zhongyan's associate, refocused the imperial exams on practical skills, less on classical artistic tastes.

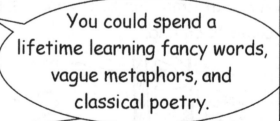

You could spend a lifetime learning fancy words, vague metaphors, and classical poetry.

But the country needs people who can think clearly and lead in crisis.

Ouyang Xiu selected his allies from among top scholars and imperial exam candidates.

Wang Anshi
No. 4 in the imperial exam of 1042

Su Xun
Proofreader in the imperial library, Secretary in local governments

His two sons passed the highest-level exam of 1057

Su Shi
Minister of Rites,
Local governor

Su Zhe
Head of various ministries and local governments

Zeng Gong
Head of various prefectures,
Court official in charge of compiling history

These scholar-officials had bumpy careers. Nearly all of them were demoted and banished in factional struggles over reform policies.

During our banishment, we use essays and poetry to express our concern about the country.

'Memorial to Yueyang Tower'
by Fan Zhongyan

A gentleman should not be pleased by external gain, and not be saddened by personal loss.

Our first concern should be the country, the last is pleasure.

不以物喜
不以己悲

先天下之忧而忧
后天下之乐而乐

His words have become a maxim encompassing the moral responsibilities of intellectuals.

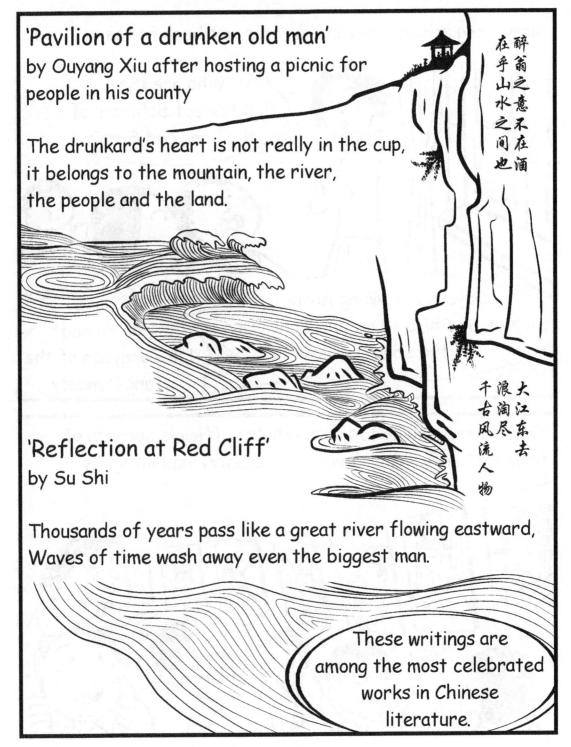

'Pavilion of a drunken old man'
by Ouyang Xiu after hosting a picnic for
people in his county

The drunkard's heart is not really in the cup,
it belongs to the mountain, the river,
the people and the land.

醉翁之意不在酒
在乎山水之間也

'Reflection at Red Cliff'
by Su Shi

大江東去
浪淘盡
千古風流人物

Thousands of years pass like a great river flowing eastward,
Waves of time wash away even the biggest man.

These writings are among the most celebrated works in Chinese literature.

Many Song scholars became famous textbook names in China.

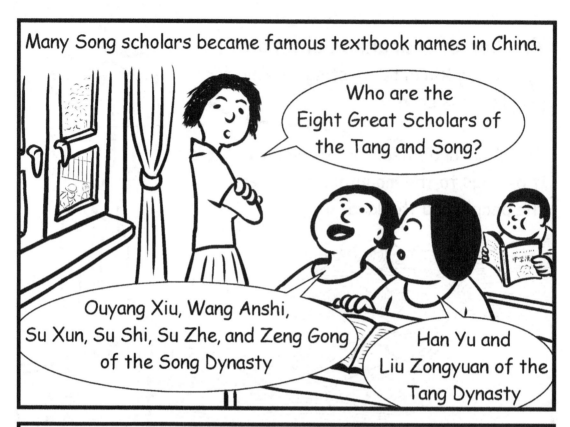

Who are the Eight Great Scholars of the Tang and Song?

Ouyang Xiu, Wang Anshi, Su Xun, Su Shi, Su Zhe, and Zeng Gong of the Song Dynasty

Han Yu and Liu Zongyuan of the Tang Dynasty

The Chinese look up to these scholar-officials because of their vast knowledge, devotion to country, and integrity.

'Along the river at the Qingming Festival'

Besides creating a lasting cultural heritage, Wang Anshi's reform also successfully revived the economy.

By the early 12th century, the Song capital, Bianjing, had become a national commercial and industrial center.

Its population surpassed 1 million, making Bianjing the largest city in the world at the time.

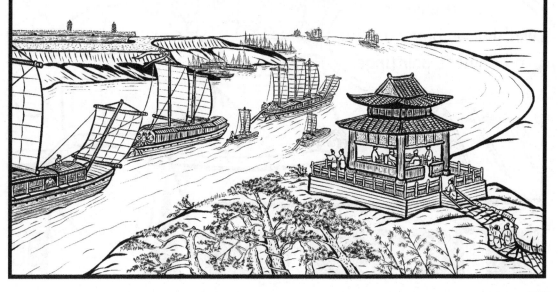

The 5.28-meter-long artwork depicts the daily life of 814 people in Bianjing and its suburbs.

street vendor

trader

traveler

official

monk

repair shop worker

boatman

coachman

sedan bearer

They conducted business everywhere: market, residential area, street, square, bridge, city gate, or countryside.

The capital of the Tang Dynasty only had two markets.

Many businesses opened at night.

For the first time, the Chinese had a nightlife.

As the first collector of 'Along the river at the Qingming Festival,' Emperor Huizong of Song was one of the most artistic rulers in history.

'Listening to the Qin' by Emperor Huizong

He was an achieved poet, painter, calligrapher, and musician.

 Huizong created a typeface, Slender Gold Type, which the Chinese are still using on computers.

One of his calligraphy works auctioned for USD 22.5 million in 2012.

During his reign, the Song population peaked around 125 million.

It's the first time the Chinese population passed 100 million thanks to the increased rice production in south China.

Huizong wanted to make his country superior to the competing Liao and Xia states, both physically and spiritually.

In Taoism, the Jade Emperor is the creator and ruler of the universe.

I'm the incarnation of his eldest son, coming to this world for the salvation of people.

The Song will officially worship the Jade Emperor each year.

Since then, the Jade Emperor has remained a popular Chinese cultural icon till this day.

Emperor Huizong continued the unfinished tasks left by his predecessors.

In 1114, his army retook the strategic Hengshan region.

To finance the war, the Song government issued national banknotes around 1120.

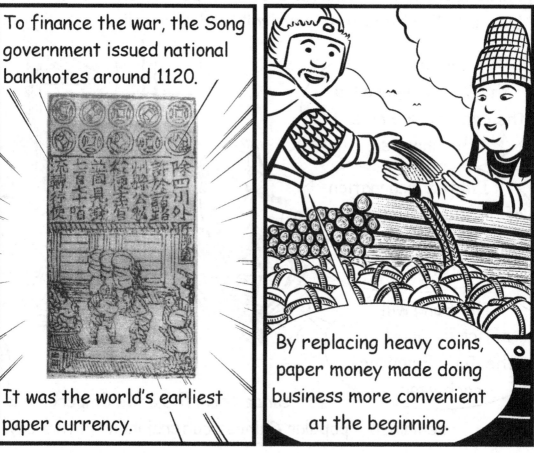

It was the world's earliest paper currency.

By replacing heavy coins, paper money made doing business more convenient at the beginning.

But increasing military spending and lack of monetary control led to an oversupply of paper money, causing major inflation.

A 1,000-coin banknote is now only worth around 10 copper coins.

Economic chaos turned into social unrest, distracting the Song from fully exploiting the victory against the Western Xia.

Loss of the Hengshan put the Western Xia in big trouble.

Your Majesty, the Song Chinese can overwhelm us anytime.

Make peace with the Song.

That'll buy us time to reorganize our troops.

I've requested help from the Liao. Any news from them?

The Liao Khitans are mobilizing a major force on their border as we speak.

Game changer: The collapse of the Liao and rise of the Jurchens

At the same time, far away from the Liao-Song-Xia deadlock, a subordinate tribe of the Liao rebelled.

Jurchen

Like the Liao Khitans before their rise, the Jurchens were stateless tribesmen who for centuries served as auxiliary troops to powerful neighbors.

In the Liao Dynasty, there were several small Jurchen clans living in northeast Asia. The Liao played one Jurchen group against another.

Appoint the Jurchen chief Wanyan Aguda as the military governor to guard our northeast border and fight other Jurchens.

In 1114, Aguda united most Jurchen tribes.

The Liao Khitans exploited us for centuries!

It's time for them to pay!

Aguda started off with less than 1,000 warriors.

In the first attack on the Liao, he rallied 2,500 men.

Following a series of small victories, the number grew to 10,000.

In 1115, Aguda founded the Jin Dynasty.

To Aguda's surprise, the mighty Liao Dynasty suddenly collapsed from within.

When the last Liao emperor led 700,000 men to crush the Jin...

Your Majesty, the nobles in our capital are plotting to seize the throne.

Let's go back to deal with the traitors!

During retreat, the Liao army suffered heavy losses in Jurchen ambushes.

To defeat the Khitans once and for all, the Jin invited the Western Xia and Song to attack the Liao from 3 sides.

Whatever you can take from the Liao will be yours!

In 1123, the Western Xia accepted the alliance and attacked the Khitans from the west.

In 1125, the Song invaded the Liao from the south.

In the same year, the Liao Dynasty ended in chaos.

In 10 years, the Jin went from a tiny tribe to a powerful state.

We've taken most of the Liao land. The surrendered Liao army is now under our command.

The Song, on the other hand, was in bad shape.

Our military never recovered from the prolonged wars against the Western Xia.

When the Liao was falling, the Song had a chance to retake the Great Wall region, but our elite troops marched all the way to south China to squelch social unrest.

Now the Jin has occupied the region. We have to negotiate buying it from them.

Emperor Huizong of Song lost his will to fight.

My son, take my throne and defend the capital.

The Song army put up fierce resistance...

...while Chinese diplomats negotiated a deal with the Jin commander.

Take these 200,000 ounces of gold and 400,000 ounces of silver, and please leave.

But a few months later in 1127, the Jin led a surprise attack with a bigger army.

Within 30 days, the Song capital fell.

We captured the Song emperor and his father Huizong...

...and the Song royal family and central government officials...

...and palace musicians, scholars, craftsmen, and female servants.

The Song Dynasty in north China, known as the Northern Song, ended.

14,000 captured Song Chinese, including 11,635 women, set off on the one-way journey.

We also have 21 of Huizong's daughters, the oldest at age 28, and the youngest at 4.

After they arrived in Jin territory, a few lucky ones served in the Jin palace.

Many were sold to brothels.

Most were tortured to death.

Emperor Huizong, once a powerful Son of Heaven who lived a life of art, died a broken man in a foreign land.

122

The incident left a scar in the memory of the Song Chinese.

Some historians believe that frequent raids from the north contributed to the custom of Chinese foot binding.

To avoid their girls being taken away, some parents bound their feet.

When the girls grew older, their feet would deform and remain small.

To the nomads, the Chinese women with bound feet were useless.

What?! They can't ride horses?!

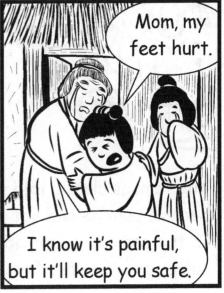

Mom, my feet hurt.

I know it's painful, but it'll keep you safe.

Readers today can have a glimpse at the eve of the fall of the Northern Song in a 14th-century novel, 'Water Margin.'

The famous classic told stories of 108 outlaws -- how they became bandits and got together to form a rebel army.
In the end, they surrendered to the government, and joined campaigns to resist foreign invaders and suppress rebellions.

Shifting south: the Southern Song

Only one Song imperial prince, Zhao Gou, son of
Emperor Huizong, escaped capture.

The court sent me
to the Jin to consolidate
a peace treaty. But before
I could reach the border,
the Jin took our capital.

Following Zhao Gou, one million refugees, including 20,000
officials and 400,000 soldiers, made it to the south.

In June 1127, Zhao Gou declared himself emperor, starting the Southern Song Dynasty.

The Jin chased me around for years, but I finally settled down in the capital Lin'an [today's Hangzhou] in 1131.

The Southern Song was in imminent danger of total collapse.

The Jin kept carrying out raids and created 2 puppet Chinese kingdoms in north China.

The Southern Song government didn't have a reliable force to defend itself.

The military becomes increasingly independent.

Two army commanders even took over the court and forced me to abdicate the throne.

After other generals rescued me, they in turn became uncontrollable.

The Southern Song military leaders insisted on fighting the Jin.

> We must use the barbarian blood to wash away our shame of losing north China!

In reality, they used the war to hold on to power.

> Many generals fake reports to boost their ranking, hide defeats, and cheat for extra state funding.

> While Jin commanders personally come to the battleground, our generals hide hundreds of miles away to command the soldiers remotely.

> Our army is so disorganized and demoralized that they will retreat on the first sign of defeat.

Widespread riots deprived the state of tax income, further weakening the Southern Song defenses.

Jin

Lin'an (Hangzhou)

Southern Song

There are several bandit groups in each province.

Each group has at least 100,000 people.

The Southern Song had no choice but to beg for peace with the Jin.

If the semi-independent generals drag on the war, we'll not only fail to recover the north, but also lose the south.

While the Southern Song was eager for peace, the Jin also had problems invading farther south.

Following the conquest of the Liao and Northern Song, our tribesmen are scattered all over the empire governing a huge Khitan and Chinese population.

Our warriors have become rich and soft after moving to places with fertile land and an easy life.

They've started to wear elegant clothes and party all night, losing their nomadic ways.

In 1141, the Jin and Southern Song signed the Treaty of Shaoxing.

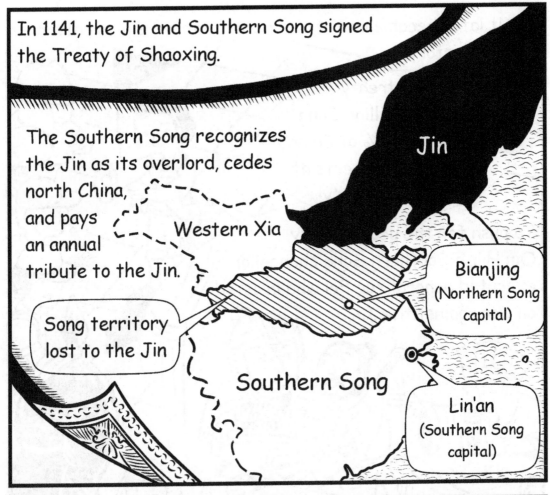

The Southern Song recognizes the Jin as its overlord, cedes north China, and pays an annual tribute to the Jin.

Jin

Western Xia

Song territory lost to the Jin

Bianjing (Northern Song capital)

Southern Song

Lin'an (Southern Song capital)

The Treaty of Shaoxing was the result of both sides realizing how little choice they had.

The Jin doesn't have the strength to conquer south China.

The Southern Song needs the peace to regroup the army and reestablish itself.

But it later became one of the most controversial events in Chinese history.

The treaty made 30 million Song Chinese, or 30% of China's population, subjects of the Jin Dynasty!

To push for the peace treaty, Qin Hui, a Southern Song chancellor executed general Yue Fei who insisted on war against the Jin.

Today, Qin Hui is widely seen as the most notorious traitor to China.

Yue Fei has become the most famous Chinese patriot.

To Chinese intellectuals, the pain of losing the Chinese heartland went back a long way.

After the fall of the Han Dynasty, nomads ruined north China.

During the Tang Dynasty, a nomadic general led the An Shi rebellion, costing 36 million lives!

In the following Five Dynasties and Ten Kingdoms, while barbarians encroached from the north, the warlords were still fighting among themselves.

They breached the Yellow River dyke to attack each other, causing 24 deadly floods within 53 years!

Now the Song has lost half of China to the Jin!

Many people see our struggles against barbarians as fighting between different dynasties.

You can't blame them. In traditional Confucian teachings, anyone can be a ruler as long as he can pacify the realm and bring peace to the people.

There is no sense of national identity. This is part of the reason why our soldiers can surrender to the enemy, our people are willing to accept foreign rule and our country is unable to expel nomad invaders.

Confucius

To guide our people and protect our nation, we need a strong culture, starting with changing Confucianism.

Neo-Confucian movement

Throughout the Song Dynasty, Chinese thinkers reformed Confucianism into new schools of thought. This is collectively known as Neo-Confucianism, the leading ideology in China for the next 800 years till 1905.

Zhou Dunyi

Zhang Zai

Chen Yi

Chen Hao

One of the most influential Neo-Confucians was a Southern Song scholar-official, Zhu Xi (1130 – 1200).

I went to school at 5, passed the imperial examination at 19, held several government positions for 10 years, and I've spent 50 years writing books and teaching in private schools.

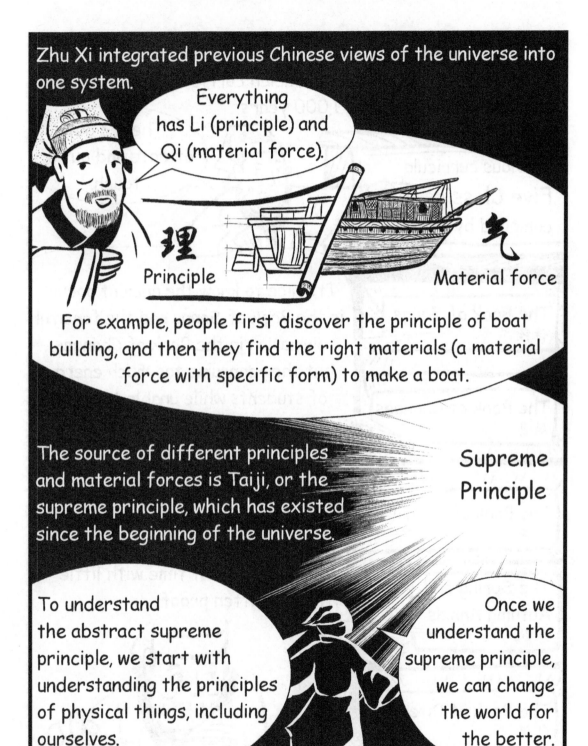

Zhu Xi integrated previous Chinese views of the universe into one system.

Everything has Li (principle) and Qi (material force).

理 Principle

气 Material force

For example, people first discover the principle of boat building, and then they find the right materials (a material force with specific form) to make a boat.

The source of different principles and material forces is Taiji, or the supreme principle, which has existed since the beginning of the universe.

Supreme Principle

To understand the abstract supreme principle, we start with understanding the principles of physical things, including ourselves.

Once we understand the supreme principle, we can change the world for the better.

Zhu Xi's major contribution to Neo-Confucianism was in reforming the traditional Confucian curricula that had been used for more than 1,000 years.

They're out of date and out of touch.

Previous curricula:
Five Classics
compiled by Confucius

The Book of Songs
诗经

The Book of Changes
周易

The Book of Documents
尚书

The Spring and Autumn Annals
春秋

The Book of Rites
礼记

It's nice to know the ancient poems in the Book of Songs and the fanciful divination in the Book of Changes, but they consume too much energy of students while unable to serve the urgent needs of our country.

The historical records in these 2 books originated in an ancient time with little written proof.

For students, the best way is to read and study.

Then meditate on how to use the acquired knowledge to guide your actions.

Meditate like Buddhist monks?

The Buddhists meditate to empty their minds and forget about this world. We sit down to think about how to make the world and people better.

In Zhu Xi's time, official schools only accepted the Five Classics.

We study the Five Classics in order to pass imperial exams.

When Zhu Xi was a local governor, he set up a private school to teach the Four Books.

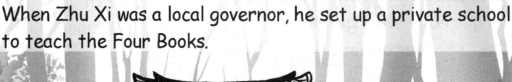

My school initially had about 10 students, mostly scholars.

Under the inspiration of Zhu Xi, other local officials and prominent scholars opened similar private academies, laying the foundation for the Four Books to become the only official version of Confucian education till 1905.

Zhu Xi also promoted Neo-Confucian ideas to households.

Previous books about rites focused on state ceremonies. I wrote this guidebook for families.

The Family Rituals

家礼

Daily etiquette

Dress code

Weddings

Funerals

Ancestor worship

For the first time, the family took its place at the center of Confucian teachings.

Zhu Xi's followers simplified his ideas into a kid's version.

The book teaches children family values as well as basic knowledge.

The Three Character Classic

三字经

Every sentence only has 3 characters. It's easy to remember.

Through grandparents, parents, and teachers, Neo-Confucian concepts were passed on in Chinese families.

Today, every Chinese knows by heart the opening lines of the Three Character Classic.

人之初 People at birth
性本善 Are naturally good
性相近 Their natures are similar
习相远 Their habits make them different

Zhu Xi is one of the most productive scholars in Chinese history.

His existing works have 13.5 million characters, including 140 chapters of Q&As with his students.

These books cover such topics as philosophy, education, governance, artistic taste, history, ritual, etiquette, and family, which are key aspects of Chinese culture.

Zhu Xi's efforts, together with other Neo-Confucians, pushed these updated Confucian values to new heights.

Traditional Chinese culture developed into its final form through the systematic study of the world, reformed curricula in schools, and books available to commoners thanks to the spread of printing.

This helped define the Chinese as 'Chinese' at a time of foreign menace.

In his later years, Zhu Xi was caught up in major political turbulence.

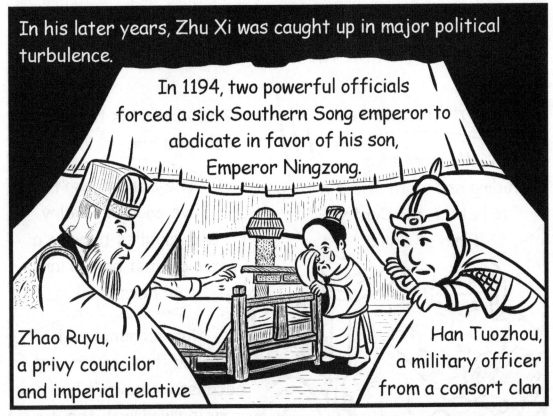

In 1194, two powerful officials forced a sick Southern Song emperor to abdicate in favor of his son, Emperor Ningzong.

Zhao Ruyu, a privy councilor and imperial relative

Han Tuozhou, a military officer from a consort clan

After the coup, both officials hired people to reinforce their positions in the court.

Upon Zhao's invitation, Zhu Xi became the emperor's personal advisor, the highest position he had ever had.

But Zhu only lasted 40 days in the court after a bitter showdown between the two rival factions.

Han Tuozhou wanted war.

Zhu Xi and his followers rebuked him.

We must stop hiding and fight the Jin to retake the Central Plain of China!

The Song doesn't have enough cavalry and supplies to wage a war against barbarians on horseback.

Our economy just started its recovery only because we haven't had any major war with the Jin for several decades.

We should first strengthen our society with Neo-Confucianism, then we can deal with the external threat.

The emperor supported Han Tuozhou.

Banish Zhao Ruyu, Zhu Xi, and 59 other Neo-Confucians from the court! Ban Neo-Confucian teachings.

A few years later in 1200, Zhu Xi died in disgrace.

With his power secured at home, Han Tuozhou led a great invasion against the Jin Dynasty in 1206.

The Jin army counterattacked.

Neither side could score a decisive victory.

Tell the Song emperor, we'll stop the war in exchange for Han Tuozhou's head...

Emperor Ningzong gave in to the Jurchen demand.

After the failed military attempt to retake north China, the Southern Song emperor needed a cultural high ground to unite leading members of society.

Restore Neo-Confucianism. All schools must use the curricula compiled by Zhu Xi.

The age of the Mongols:

The Mongol Empire

1206 - 1368

When the Southern Song and Jin engaged in a war of attrition, another event was taking place in the remote northern grasslands.

A nomadic tribe was uniting the Central Asian plateau into a confederation, known as the Mongol Empire.

In 1206, their leader took the title Genghis Khan, or the Lord of Lords.

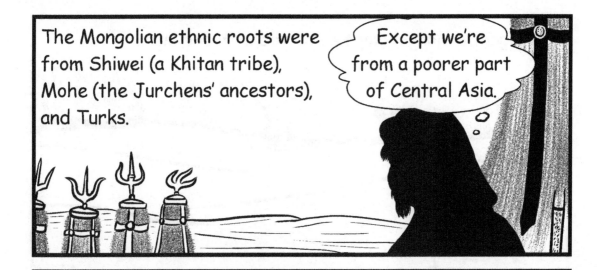

The Mongolian ethnic roots were from Shiwei (a Khitan tribe), Mohe (the Jurchens' ancestors), and Turks.

Except we're from a poorer part of Central Asia.

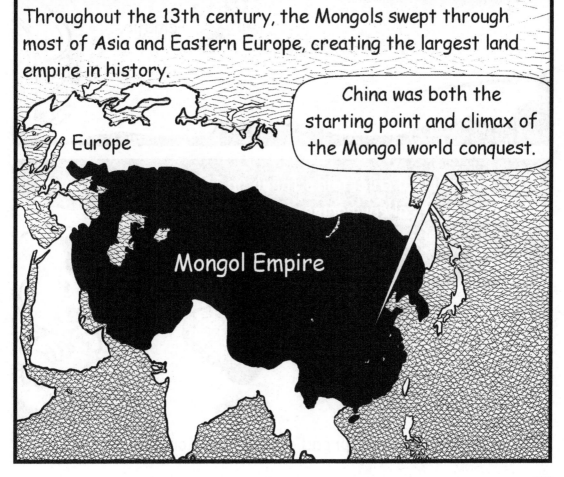

Throughout the 13th century, the Mongols swept through most of Asia and Eastern Europe, creating the largest land empire in history.

China was both the starting point and climax of the Mongol world conquest.

Europe

Mongol Empire

The gigantic Mongol empire started with one man...

...Temujin.

Born into a tribal chieftain's family in 1162, Temujin grew up in a toxic political environment.

Tribal wars were widespread among the Mongols.

Temujin saw his father murdered by a rival tribe when he was a boy.

His father's former ally captured him but he escaped with his life.

His wife was kidnapped to become another man's wife.

In his battle for survival, Temujin fought over 100 tribes, including his former ally and best friend since childhood.

The life of struggle, betrayal, and revenge made Temujin ruthless.

There is no greater joy than killing one's enemies, seizing all their belongings, and taking their wives and daughters.

Temujin's ascent to power began with working for the Jin Dynasty.

In 1195, he helped the Jin suppress rebellions of other tribes.

Temujin, you've served the Jin well. Now I appoint you an army officer commanding 100 men.

Later, he joined a tribe that was a major ally of the Jin.

Temujin gradually gained strength and waited...

The Jin Dynasty had tried to strangle any Mongol ambition in its infancy.

Every 2 years we select a Mongol tribe to attack.

The order is to cut off the thumbs of every man in that tribe, so he can't hold a weapon.

Any resistance, kill them.

The Jin's preemptive policies bred deep hatred among the Mongols.

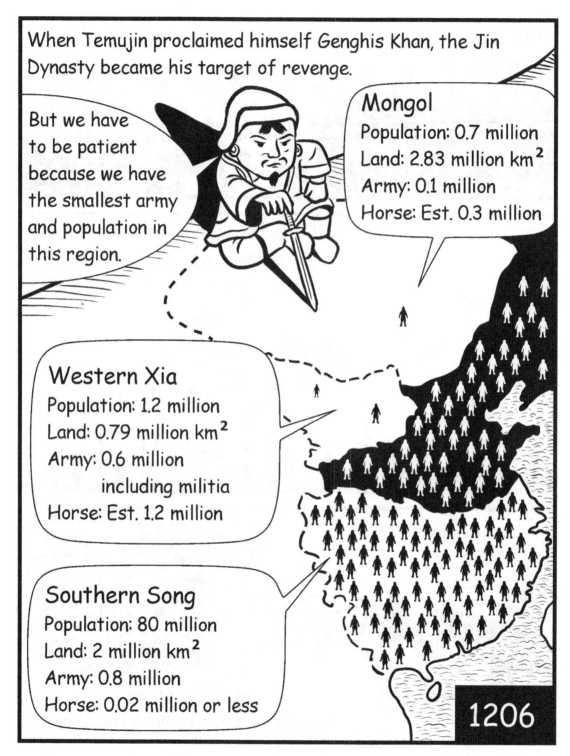

When Temujin proclaimed himself Genghis Khan, the Jin Dynasty became his target of revenge.

But we have to be patient because we have the smallest army and population in this region.

Mongol
Population: 0.7 million
Land: 2.83 million km^2
Army: 0.1 million
Horse: Est. 0.3 million

Western Xia
Population: 1.2 million
Land: 0.79 million km^2
Army: 0.6 million
            including militia
Horse: Est. 1.2 million

Southern Song
Population: 80 million
Land: 2 million km^2
Army: 0.8 million
Horse: 0.02 million or less

1206

Starting point of the Mongol world conquest

In 1211, the Mongols rode out to invade the Jin. The campaign was a tremendous gamble for Genghis Khan.

Mongol capital Karakorum

We mobilized over 90,000 cavalry for this campaign, leaving only 2,000 guarding the Mongol home base.

Mongol-Jin border

Jin Central Capital (Beijing)

Our 400,000 Jurchen warriors are waiting for you!

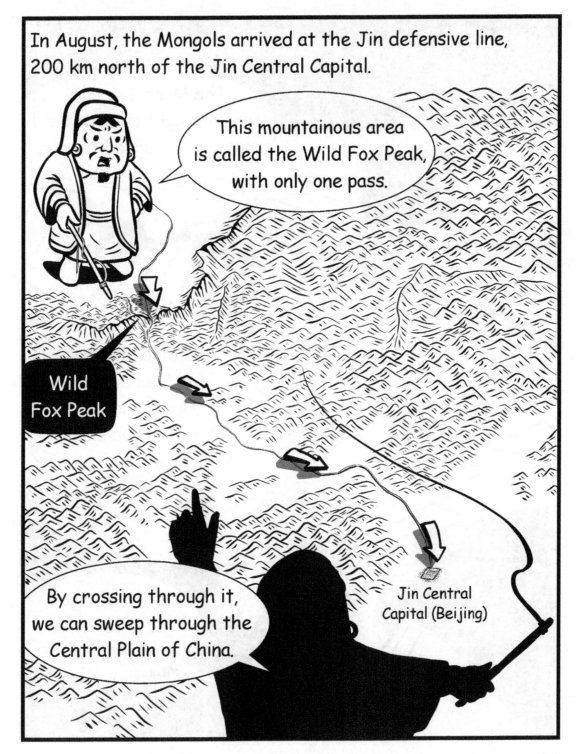

On the day of battle, Genghis led his men to the pass.

They attacked.

Wave after wave...

Arrows and rocks started pouring down on them.

Many men fell.

The Mongols just keep coming.

Send an order to bring over more troops stationed on other mountains!

We must hold the line!

Suddenly, chaos broke out amidst the Jin army.

The Mongols have come from behind us!

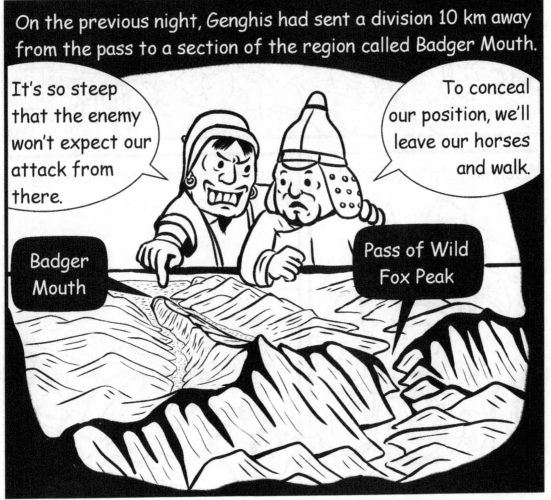

On the previous night, Genghis had sent a division 10 km away from the pass to a section of the region called Badger Mouth.

It's so steep that the enemy won't expect our attack from there.

To conceal our position, we'll leave our horses and walk.

Badger Mouth

Pass of Wild Fox Peak

While the main attack at the mountain pass attracted the attention of all Jin units, the Mongol division climbed the slopes and fortified walls...

...seized lightly guarded towers...

...and ran toward the pass along the mountain ridges.

The surprise attack took the pressure off the Mongol cavalry. They broke through the mountain pass.

The Jin central command and supplies were destroyed.

Terrified Jin soldiers left on the mountains could only watch.

Most fled.

The Mongol cavalry pursued, killing everyone on the run.

This campaign, known as the Battle of Badger Mouth, was one of the bloodiest battles in history. The Jin lost nearly 400,000 defensive troops.

The Mongols considered it the most important victory in consolidating the Mongol Empire.

The Mongol victory made the Jin crumble.

The Western Xia agreed to a military alliance with the Mongols and began a decade-long war with the Jin.

The Jin attacked the Southern Song, hoping to regain some territorial and financial losses caused by the Mongols.

A few years after the Battle of Badger Mouth, the Jin was isolated, fighting a war on 3 fronts.

The Mongols, on the other hand, secured regional supremacy, marking the beginning of its world conquest.

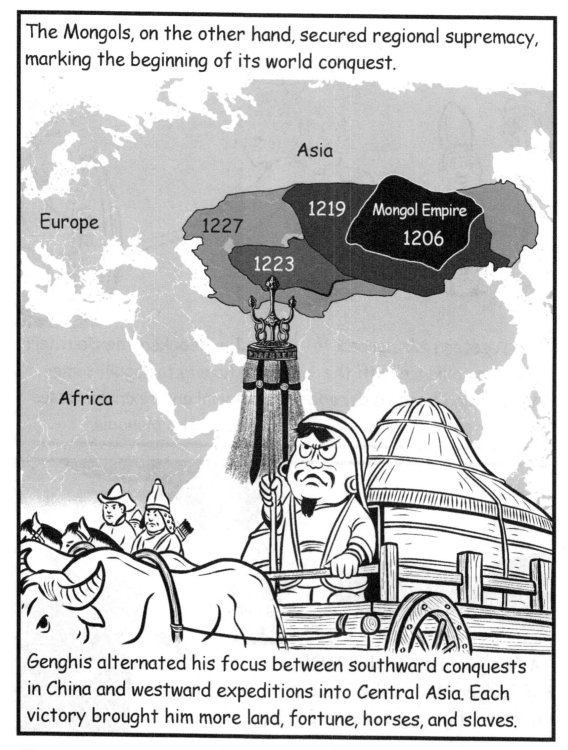

Genghis alternated his focus between southward conquests in China and westward expeditions into Central Asia. Each victory brought him more land, fortune, horses, and slaves.

Around 1224, a new development in China alarmed Genghis.

The Western Xia openly resisted his rule.

The Mongols are working us to death!

First they drew us into war with the Jin!

Then they demanded our troops for campaigns against Islamic countries in the west.

The Xia, Jin, and Song should fight together against the Mongols, not each other!

Under the initiative of the Xia Tanguts, the wars between these 3 states in China stopped.

In 1226, Genghis invaded the Western Xia.

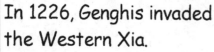

The Tanguts resisted fiercely.

In a battle besieging the Xia capital, Genghis suddenly came to his end.

Some believed he had received a fatal wound from an arrow.

My great Khan, you can't die. The Western Xia ruler just said they would surrender.

Ögedei, the third son of Genghis Khan

Don't announce my death until they submit. Then kill every single one of them...

One more thing, you must destroy the Jin.

Send an army through the Southern Song to attack the Jin capital from behind.

Mongol Empire

Jin

Southern Song

In 1227, Genghis Khan died.

The last Western Xia emperor surrendered shortly thereafter...

Soon it was clear that the Jin couldn't hold on much longer.

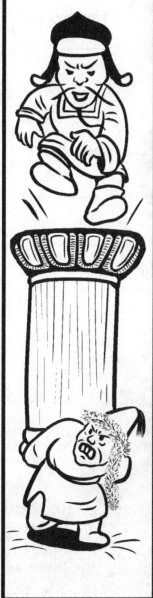

The Southern Song then joined the Mongols, hoping to recapture its long-lost land in north China.

In 1234, the last Jurchen defense collapsed, ending the Jin Dynasty.

After the destruction of the Western Xia and Jin, the Southern Song became the next target of Mongol conquest.

Mongol Empire

Former Jin territory

Former Western Xia territory

Southern Song

In 1235, the Song-Mongol war broke out.

To terrify people into submission, the Mongols frequently massacred entire city populations. In the city of Chengdu alone, 1.4 million residents were brutally killed.

But the Mongol army couldn't destroy the Chinese defensive line.

We've invaded them every year for 3 years.

Our fast moving cavalry isn't made for slow siege, muddy riverside battle, or naval war.

Redirect our main forces to westward campaigns.

Let's deal with the Southern Song later.

Asia

Europe

Mongol Empire
1237

Southern Song

Africa

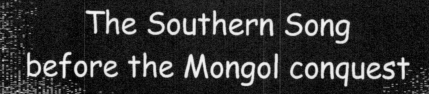

The Southern Song before the Mongol conquest

With the Mongol attack temporarily halted, the Southern Song wasted no time in building up its military and economic strength.

Besides a huge infantry, we have a strong navy with 52,000 marines and 22 battle fleets.

Our paddle-wheel ships are armed with catapults that can launch fire bombs.

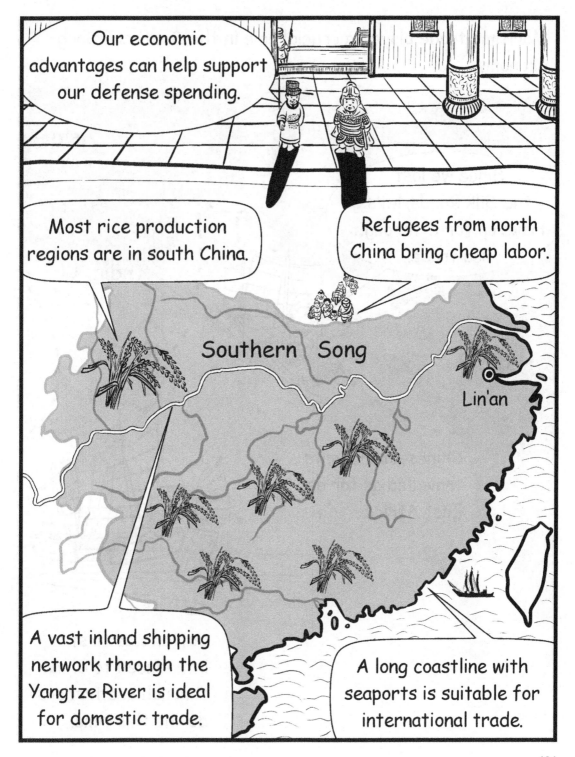

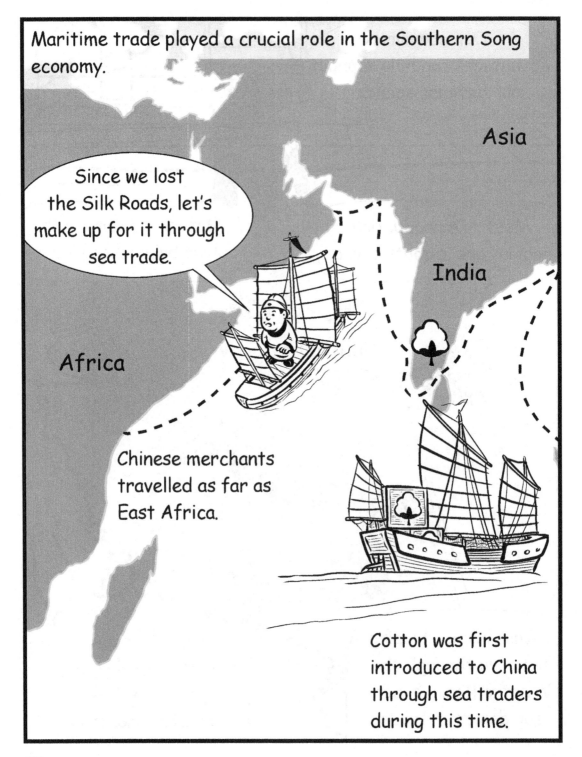

Maritime trade played a crucial role in the Southern Song economy.

Since we lost the Silk Roads, let's make up for it through sea trade.

Asia

India

Africa

Chinese merchants travelled as far as East Africa.

Cotton was first introduced to China through sea traders during this time.

Quanzhou became the world largest port at the time. It was later known as the starting point of the Maritime Silk Roads.

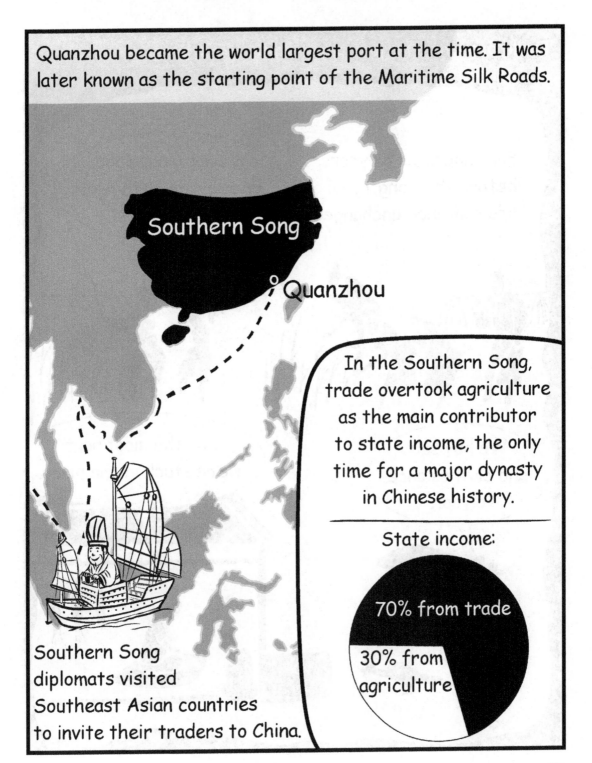

Southern Song

Quanzhou

Southern Song diplomats visited Southeast Asian countries to invite their traders to China.

In the Southern Song, trade overtook agriculture as the main contributor to state income, the only time for a major dynasty in Chinese history.

State income:

70% from trade

30% from agriculture

Population migration and commercial expansion led to rapid growth of cities.

Cities with population above 100,000

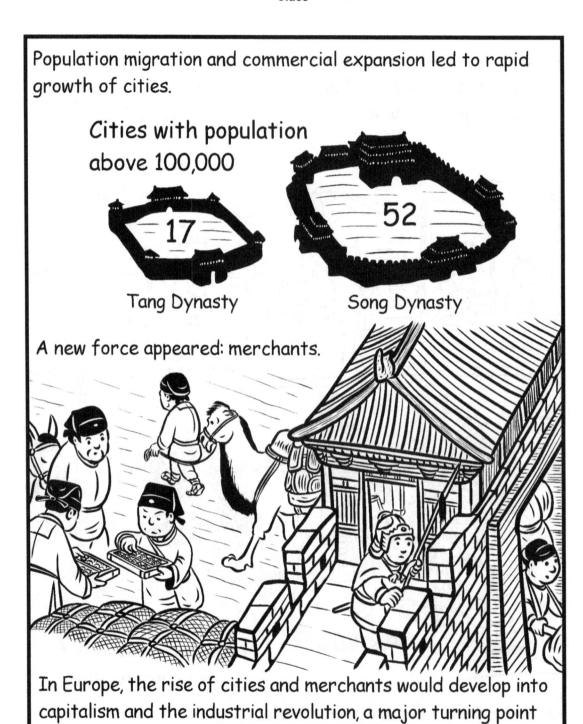

17

Tang Dynasty

52

Song Dynasty

A new force appeared: merchants.

In Europe, the rise of cities and merchants would develop into capitalism and the industrial revolution, a major turning point in history. In China, a similar rise also greatly impacted society.

The Southern Song merchants came to cities from different parts of the country. For those who had connections with officials, there were many quick ways to make a fortune.

Trade in state monopoly goods, such as rice, salt, liquor, tea, spice

Military supplies to border troops

Money-lending to the government

Most other merchants engaged in all kinds of wholesale or retail businesses.

The ruling elites often looked down on merchants.

These people buy and sell things made by others.

Everything they do is for profit, contributing little to the state.

We must curb their influence, for example, we shouldn't allow candidates from merchant families to take the imperial exams.

However, there was little that could stop this new force from changing the political landscape.

I hired a good tutor for my children. I'll register them under a relative's name, who is not a businessman, so they can take the exams to become officials one day.

To better protect their interests, merchants organized themselves into powerful guilds, or chambers of commerce. These associations dealt with the government in matters such as taxation, law enforcement, and public obligations.

Guilds played a key role in the operations of their members.

All business between a member and his client must be conducted through the guild.

Each member must be honest, loyal, and reliable.

Members can also come to the guild for help, such as loans.

With the expansion of the merchant class in cities, what used to be reserved for royalty became available to ordinary people. There were plenty of places to go and things to do.

People could go to training schools to learn calligraphy, painting, poetry, essays, opera, music, dance, or performance.

For kids, there were singing schools, and places to play with puppets or toys.

The Mongols are back!

Before trade, urbanization, and new social classes could push China onto a completely different track, the Mongols were back, two decades after their initial conflict with the Southern Song. This time, they were much stronger.

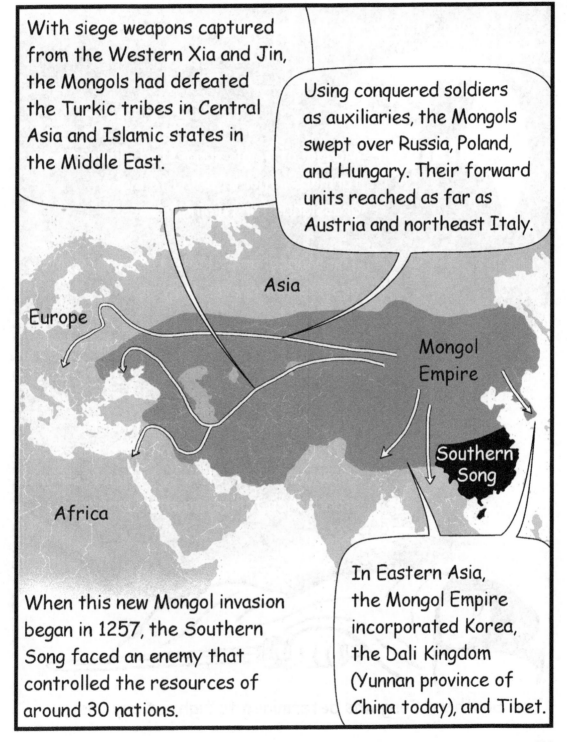

With siege weapons captured from the Western Xia and Jin, the Mongols had defeated the Turkic tribes in Central Asia and Islamic states in the Middle East.

Using conquered soldiers as auxiliaries, the Mongols swept over Russia, Poland, and Hungary. Their forward units reached as far as Austria and northeast Italy.

Asia

Europe

Mongol Empire

Southern Song

Africa

When this new Mongol invasion began in 1257, the Southern Song faced an enemy that controlled the resources of around 30 nations.

In Eastern Asia, the Mongol Empire incorporated Korea, the Dali Kingdom (Yunnan province of China today), and Tibet.

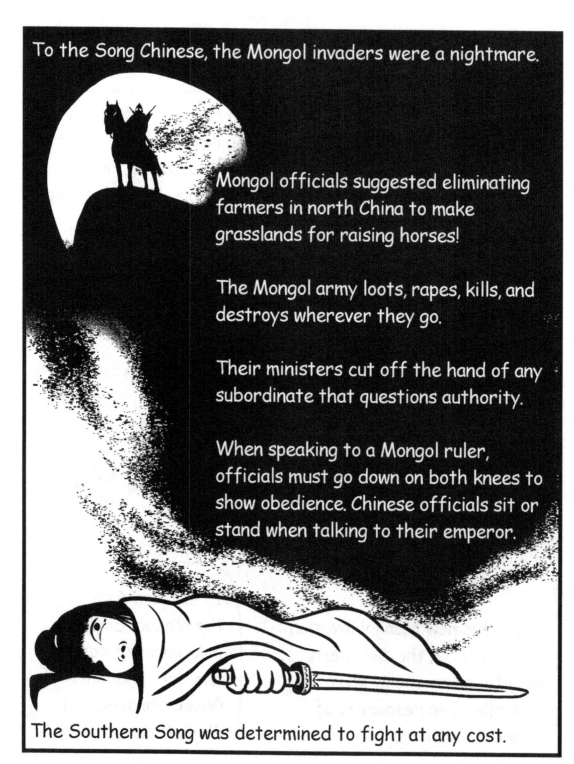

To the Song Chinese, the Mongol invaders were a nightmare.

Mongol officials suggested eliminating farmers in north China to make grasslands for raising horses!

The Mongol army loots, rapes, kills, and destroys wherever they go.

Their ministers cut off the hand of any subordinate that questions authority.

When speaking to a Mongol ruler, officials must go down on both knees to show obedience. Chinese officials sit or stand when talking to their emperor.

The Southern Song was determined to fight at any cost.

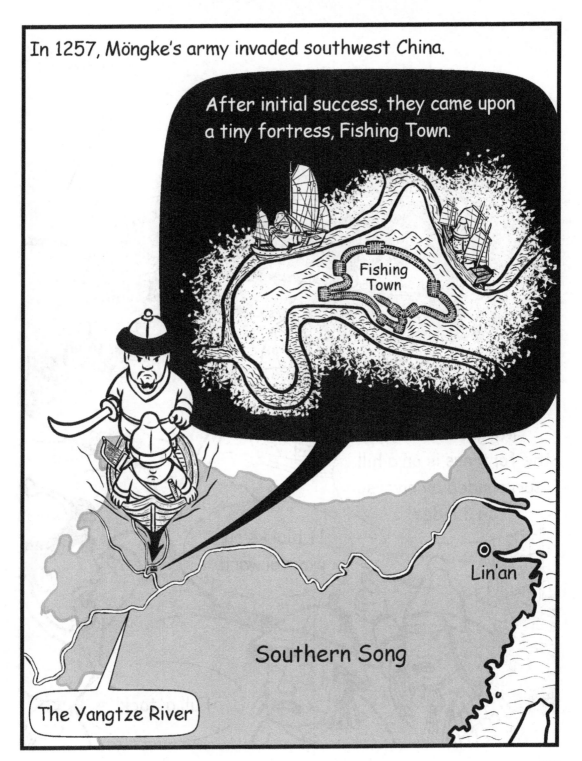

The little town held out.

And it held out against more than 200 assaults in 36 years till the very end of the Southern Song. The Fishing Town became a legend, not only for its resilience but also for killing Möngke Khan in 1259, triggering the break-up of the Mongol Empire!

Upon the news arriving that Möngke died while campaigning against the Southern Song, Ariq Böke asked all Mongol leaders to pause their worldwide conquests and return to the capital.

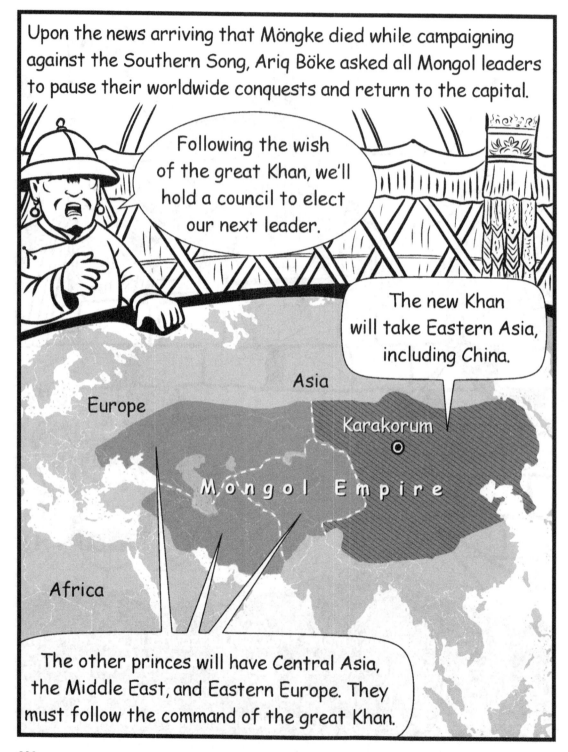

Following the wish of the great Khan, we'll hold a council to elect our next leader.

The new Khan will take Eastern Asia, including China.

Asia

Europe

Karakorum

Mongol Empire

Africa

The other princes will have Central Asia, the Middle East, and Eastern Europe. They must follow the command of the great Khan.

When will the council be ready?

We're still waiting for your older brother, Kublai.

Kublai didn't show up. Instead, he claimed to be the great Khan in his own territory in 1260.

Karakorum

Xanadu

M o n g o l   E m p i r e

Southern Song

In response, Ariq Böke started the great council.

Kublai is drowning himself in their 'Chinese-ness.' Now he openly betrays our law of election.

Today, you vote for me, you vote for our Mongol way of life!

Ariq Böke!

Ariq Böke!

Ariq Böke!

A civil war broke out.

Relatives from other Mongol territories joined the fight.

Kublai spent 4 years subduing his younger brother...

...and his entire reign of 30 years to fight other Mongol contenders to his throne.

The Mongol Empire divided into 4 independent realms with individual Khans, greatly weakening Mongol power.

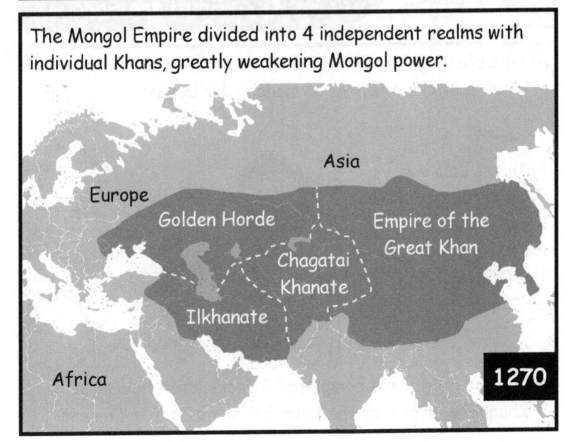

Kublai Khan lost control of the western Mongol Empire and counted on Eastern Asia, especially China, to secure his position.

Once we conquer the Southern Song and control its resources and manpower, other Mongol territories stand no chance against us.

Southern Song

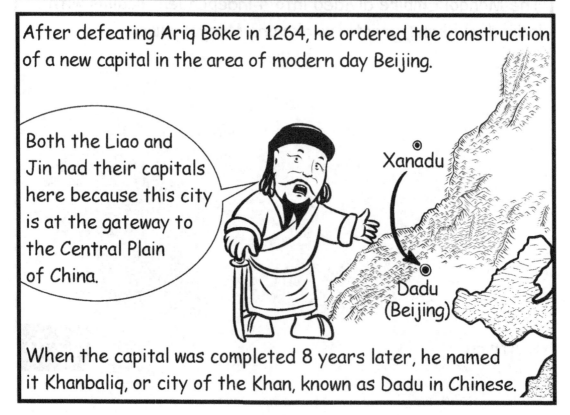

After defeating Ariq Böke in 1264, he ordered the construction of a new capital in the area of modern day Beijing.

Both the Liao and Jin had their capitals here because this city is at the gateway to the Central Plain of China.

Xanadu

Dadu (Beijing)

When the capital was completed 8 years later, he named it Khanbaliq, or city of the Khan, known as Dadu in Chinese.

To make his conquest more 'acceptable' to the Song Chinese, Kublai Khan adopted a Chinese name for his empire:

The Yuan Dynasty
1271 – 1368

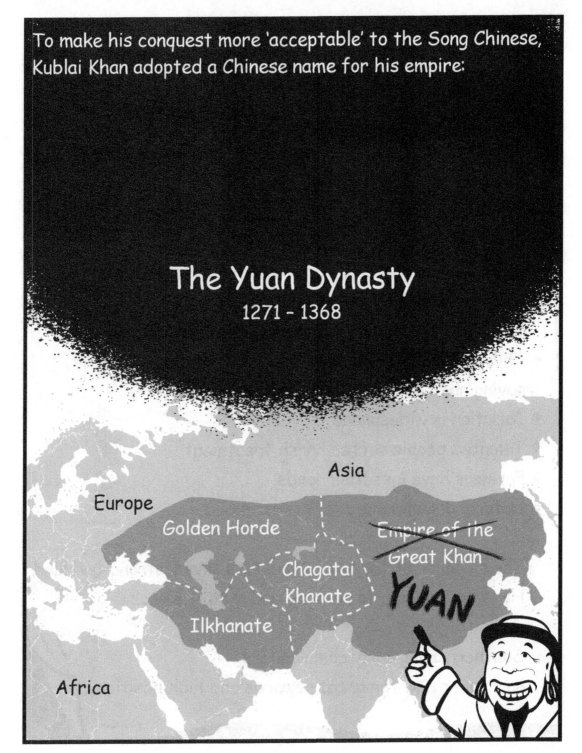

Asia

Europe

Golden Horde

~~Empire of the Great Khan~~

Chagatai Khanate

YUAN

Ilkhanate

Africa

As emperor of China, Kublai made an announcement to the south.

It's time to reunify China.
Our army is coming to save you from criminals.

- The Southern Song is plagued with corrupt officials.
- They seize all business opportunities,
  take huge bribes, and fill the court with their own kind.
- They distance themselves from the people,
  paying no attention to the alarming situation.
- Inflation is widespread,
- Talented people suffer harsh treatment,
- Farmers have lost their lands,
- Natural disasters are left unattended.

The Emperor of the Yuan Dynasty is smart, strong, and kind.
He is determined to restore order to the realm.

Southern Song army commanders,
surrender now for great rewards and high positions.

Battle of Xiangyang

In 1268, the Yuan Mongols launched their final assault. They met tough resistance, especially at the city of Xiangyang.

In battle, we need 100,000 arrows each day.

With supplies running low, our special units carry out night raids to take arrows from the Mongols.

There is a problem!

Before the barbarians came, most people in the surrounding area moved into the city, some leaving their dogs behind.

So?!

Now there are thousands of dogs out there.

When we went out at night, some dogs barked, revealing our position.

Can't you use bamboo cages to trap these dogs?

That way you can bring back arrows and extra food.

With various ingenious defensive plans, Xiangyang stood fast for years.

As the siege went on, the Yuan army severed the last land connection to the city.

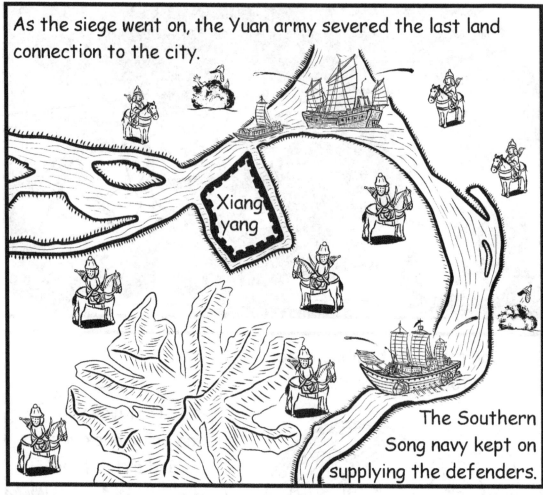

Xiang yang

The Southern Song navy kept on supplying the defenders.

Kublai Khan was getting increasingly impatient.

Build 5,000 ships and train 70,000 marines to block their river supply-lines!

The new Yuan naval force disrupted the Song reinforcements.

Less and less supplies went through in the last year of the resistance.

Every day, watchtower soldiers looked out on the river for a sign of their navy.

SONG

What is that?

They fired test shots on a small city across the river from Xiangyang.

Giant stones pulverized the city to the ground.

The Mongols killed its entire population.

In March 1273, Xiangyang surrendered after 5 years of siege.

The Yangtze River was open to large Yuan fleets.

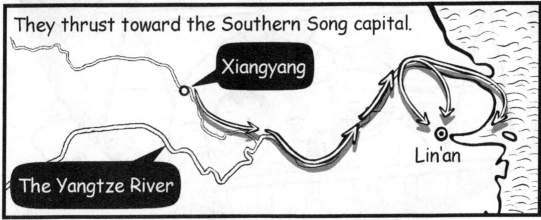

They thrust toward the Southern Song capital.

Xiangyang

The Yangtze River

Lin'an

In 1276, Lin'an fell.

The 5-year-old Southern Song emperor, in the arms of his grandmother, surrendered to the Yuan army.

Last stand of the Song Chinese

Some escaped, including a scholar-official, Lu Xiufu, and 2 imperial princes. Lu and other Song loyalists put a 7-year-old prince on the throne, gathering forces while retreating south.

But the child emperor soon died of illness during constant flight.

His younger brother became the last emperor of the Song Dynasty.

In 1279, the remaining Southern Song resistance of 200,000 men and women regrouped onto a fleet of 1,000 ships.

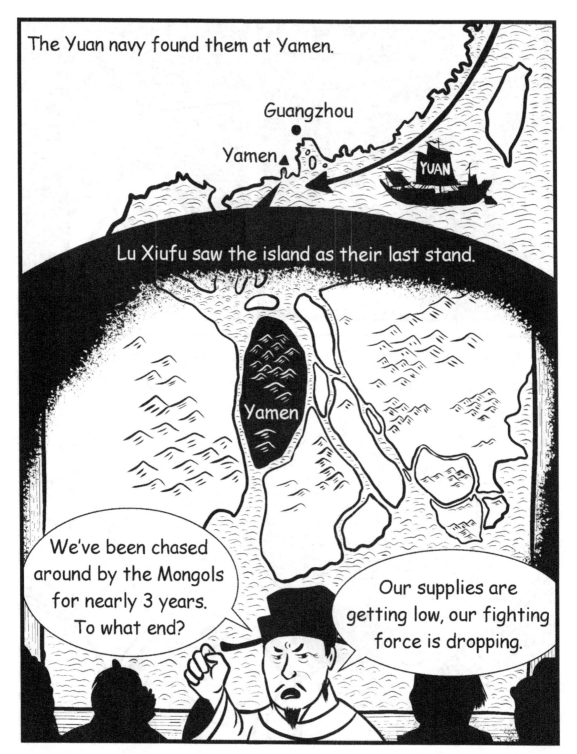

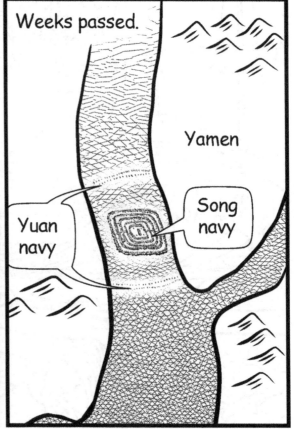

Knowing all was lost, Lu Xiufu went to the emperor.

Today our country is destroyed. Let's not bear even more pain by surrendering.

Lu Xiufu tied the 8-year-old crying boy and the imperial seal to his back...

...and jumped into the sea, ending the Song Dynasty.

The battle of Yamen cost
the Song Chinese
100,000 lives.

The Mongol conquest had disrupted
agriculture, causing widespread famine.
The population of China fell from 140 million to 60 million.

Life under Mongol rule

The Yuan Mongols were not interested in looking after the newly conquered subjects. After grabbing their own share of territory, the Mongols let the land distribution run its course.

The Yuan has 363 million mu* of farmland.

18% of farmland to reward 150 Mongol nobles and officials, and more than 4,000 Buddhist temples

5% for 120 state-owned farms, mainly providing food for the military

* 1 mu = 0.165 acres = 666.67 m2

53% controlled by tens of thousands of large landowners, mostly in south China

During the Mongol onslaught, our family hired private armies for self-defense.

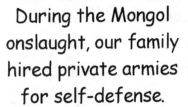

After the Song collapsed, we surrendered in order to keep our farmland.

24% shared by 13 million farmer households

Now we're running 1 million mu of land with 10,000 tenant families working for us.

Large landowners in the Yuan period could amass millions, even tens of millions mu of land, while the wealthy landowners in the Song Dynasty only had tens of thousands.

Large landowners in the Song Dynasty

Large landowners in the Yuan Dynasty

The extreme concentration of land was the worst in history, forcing most farmers to become tenants.

We pay rent with half of our harvest.

In bad years, we'll be in debt, starve, or even have to sell our children.

To ensure Mongol superiority over the Chinese majority, Kublai Khan divided his people into 4 social classes.

1 Mongols

2 Miscellaneous ethnic groups, including Uyghurs, Tanguts, Tibetans, Central Asians, Middle Eastern, and Europeans

Let me clarify the classification in a way you can understand.

3 Northern Chinese, including Khitans and Jurchens

4 Southern barbarians, or Chinese of the former Southern Song

If a Mongol hits a Chinese, the Chinese can't fight back.

If the Chinese is beaten to death, the Mongol is only responsible for the funeral costs.

Besides imposing a semi-military rule on the Chinese, Kublai Khan tried to curb Chinese cultural influence.

To replace Chinese as the official language, I commissioned a Tibetan Buddhist leader to invent a new writing system.

Tibetan lamas will manage all religious affairs.

Chinese   new script

Chögyal Phagpa

Yang Rin-chen-skyabs

To pay for new Buddhist temples, we're digging out treasure from over 100 tombs of Song emperors, royal families, and officials.

A famous cultural figure of the Yuan Dynasty was Guan Hanqing.

He is considered by many to be the greatest playwright in Chinese history.

He wrote around 60 titles, with 14 still commonly read today.

Injustice to Dou E
窦娥冤

Saving the Prostitute
赵盼儿风月
救风尘

In his work, Guan indirectly expressed his anger over Mongol rule.

I'm a tough little copper pea that so many have tried to crack open by steaming, boiling, hammering, and stir-frying.

You can knock out my teeth, mess up my face, cripple my legs, and break my arms, but you can never stop me.

Marco Polo

In his distrust of Chinese scholars, Kublai Khan used people from Central Asia, the Middle East, and Europe to manage the economy and collect tax.

Many foreigners came to work in China, including a Venetian merchant and his son Marco Polo.

Marco Polo lived, worked and traveled in China for 17 years.

The Yuan court once put me in charge of salt production in a city in south China.

Dadu (Beijing)

Yuan

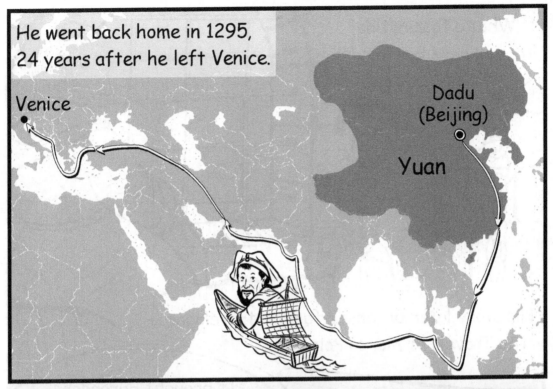

What a fascinating life you have led! I must write a book.

His story later became a famous travelogue -- 'The Travels of Marco Polo.'

The book has 4 parts.

It brought Europeans their first insight into Chinese politics and people's daily lives.

1. Journey to China

2. China and the Yuan court

3. Neighboring countries to China

4. Wars between different Mongol territories

The original manuscript was lost. Later copying and translating added many errors, which fueled growing suspicion over Marco Polo's tale. Europeans of the time gave the book a nickname: 'The Million.'

The book is full of huge numbers and very hard for us to believe.

Listen to this.

Ha! Ha!

The city of Hangzhou has 12,000 bridges, over 1 million people, and 1.6 million houses!

The Chinese emperor used to live there, and he had thousands of wives, and he raised 20,000 orphans every year.

In a nearby port, there are 15,000 ships docking at 1 wharf.

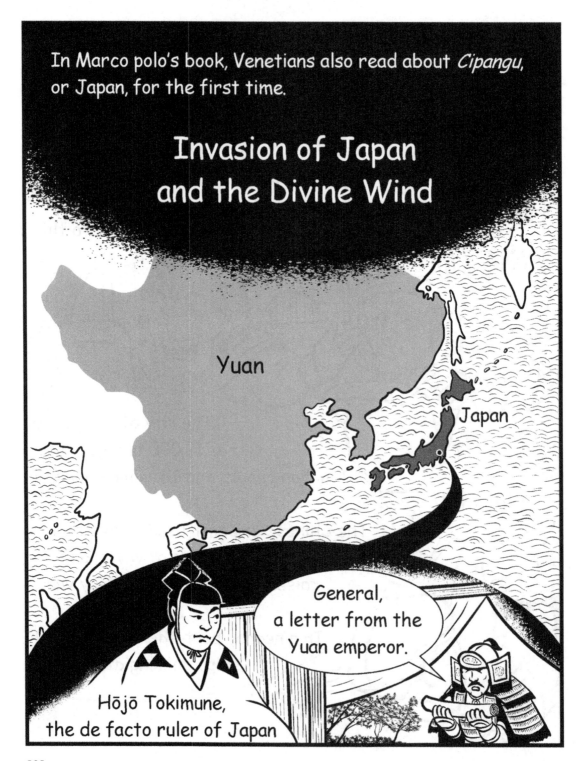

In Marco polo's book, Venetians also read about *Cipangu*, or Japan, for the first time.

Invasion of Japan and the Divine Wind

Yuan

Japan

General, a letter from the Yuan emperor.

Hōjō Tokimune, the de facto ruler of Japan

Send a tribute mission to pay your respects to the Yuan emperor.

The world is one family, and you'll be treated like a son.

Nobody wants war.

Japan didn't submit to the threat.

Kublai Khan answered with a major invasion into Japan, shortly after conquering the Southern Song.

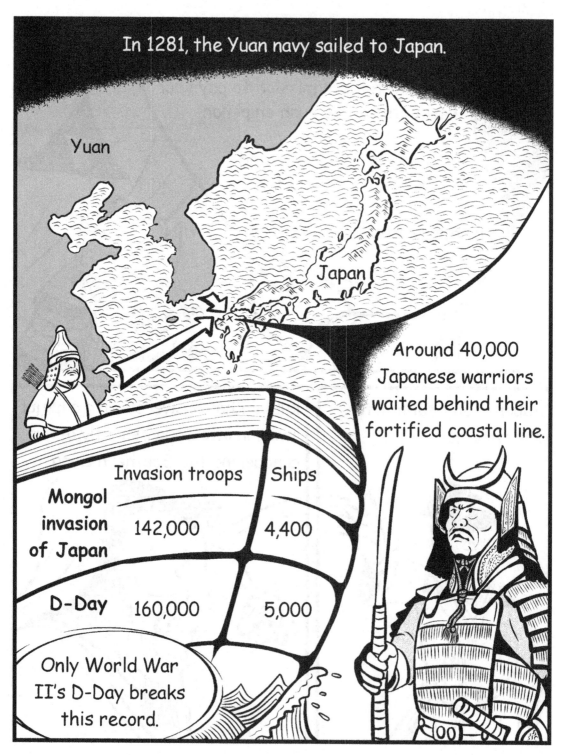

In 1281, the Yuan navy sailed to Japan.

Yuan

Japan

Around 40,000 Japanese warriors waited behind their fortified coastal line.

	Invasion troops	Ships
Mongol invasion of Japan	142,000	4,400
D-Day	160,000	5,000

Only World War II's D-Day breaks this record.

After fighting for 2 months, the main Yuan army still couldn't land.

YUAN

Then came a huge typhoon, the famous *Kamikaze*. Nearly 80% of the Yuan soldiers died.

Less than 200 ships survived.

Kublai Khan immediately planned another attack.

Find me more soldiers and ships!

Only his own death in 1294 could stop him.

The Mongol invasion interrupted official trade between China and Japan. Many Japanese traders used farmers, fishermen, and soldiers for smuggling, some becoming pirates.

The problem of Japanese pirates lasted well into the succeeding dynasty.

Quick decline

Kublai left his successors an empire with an old question.

How to share power between central and local governments without leading to disunity?

A Chinese dynasty often built a strong central government and treated local governments as subjects.

Kublai followed Mongol tradition and shared power with family and friends.

This decentralization led to the rise of local powers and weakened the central government, threatening the existence of the Yuan Dynasty.

After Kublai, the second Yuan ruler could no longer wage wars.

Early wars with neighboring states have brought high inflation, causing small riots to spread.

Call off all war preparations and sue for peace with western Mongol territories.

YUAN

Nevertheless, the Yuan started its quick decline, marked by internal conflicts and unstable reigns.

Then natural disasters struck.

Droughts

Floods

Famines

The Black Death broke out in western Mongol territories in the 14th century, severing all trade with the Yuan.

Over 75 million people worldwide died from the pandemic.

In 1351 rebellions started in several regions of south China, where the tax burdens were the highest.

In just 17 years, a Chinese rebel army captured the Yuan capital, ending Mongol rule of China.

The Yuan made 50% of its tax income from the former Southern Song, which accounted for less than 10% of Yuan territory.

Chinese civilization survived Mongol rule, but at a high cost.

After the Yuan Dynasty, China's priority was to rebuild its social order and cultural identity, while losing its originality and curiosity, which were crucial for the country to face what was yet to come.

The Chinese became protective of what they believed was Chinese, rejected what they thought was foreign, and drifted away from their great tradition -- that of embracing other cultures to enrich their own.

At the same time, explorers like Marco Polo contributed to high demand for Chinese goods in Europe. They also brought back printing, the compass, and gunpowder. Exchange of goods and knowledge made important contributions to the Age of Discovery, a bridge between the European Middle Ages and its Modern era.

When China clashed with western countries in the 19th century, it found itself short of ideas to move the country and its people forward. In their own words, the Chinese had to face "a time of change that we have not seen in thousands of years."

Understanding CHINA through Comics

Volume 4 coming in December 2014

Table of Contents

About the author

Liu Jing was born and raised in the era of opening-up Beijing. He is a successful Chinese artist and entrepreneur who works regularly with international clients and has made many friends through his work and travels inside and outside his native country.

Time and again, he is asked questions as others seek to understand China:

What makes the Chinese 'Chinese'?

How have the Chinese people and their culture evolved and changed over the millennia?

Why do Chinese appear genetically wired to think there should be a single, unified China?

Are Chinese people religious?

With this English comic book about Chinese history, Liu Jing hopes to put these questions and the answers into historical context: for his son, his friends both near and far, and for anyone who has even a passing interest in understanding what China is and from whence it came.

CPSIA information can be obtained at www.ICGtesting.com
Printed in the USA
LVOW03s2239080215

426215LV00005B/49/P

9 780983 830856